The I-70 Strangler An Anthology of True Crime

Ruth Canton

Published by Trellis Publishing, 2021.

THE I-70 STRANGLER AN ANTHOLOGY OF TRUE CRIME

First edition. June 29, 2021.

Copyright © 2021 Ruth Canton.

ISBN: 979-8224295036

Written by Ruth Canton.

The I-70 Strangler

Ruth Canton

TABLE OF CONTENTS

Table of Contents

THE I-70 STRANGLER

EVELYN HARTLEY
JODI HUISENTRUIT
BRITTANEE DREXEL
PATRICIA MEEHAN

Early Life

On April 7, 1947, anesthesiologist Herbert Baumeister Sr. and his wife Elizabeth welcomed their first child, Herbert Richard Baumeister. The family lived in the Butler-Tarkington neighborhood of Indiana, and three more children were added to the family; Barbra, Brad, and Richard. Herb, the oldest son, soon found himself in a cramped house with his parents and siblings, and grew to hate the lack of freedom he enjoyed when he was the only child. Fortunately for the family, Herbert Sr. was enjoying a continually lucrative career, and was soon able to make enough money to afford a bigger house in the more affluent neighborhood of Washington Township, north of Indianapolis. Herb was thrilled. While he did enjoy doting on his younger siblings, he was grateful for the added space. He could now breathe a little easier.

Herbert Sr. was a chronic workaholic, and spent extended periods of times away from home. The children never interacted much with him, but he ensured that they were taken care of and healthy. His son, Herb, was funny as a young boy, cracking jokes and setting up countless practical jokes that had the family laughing. Herb was present when his family was still financially unstable, and did not indulge in the newfound luxury in the same way that his siblings did. He worked hard and diligently, and was praised by his teachers. He was popular among his friends, always making them laugh. This all changed when he hit puberty.

Herb's personality began to change quite subtly. He worked hard, maintained the same friends, and still possessed some of the charm from his childhood years. However, his interests began to shift, and his practical jokes started getting more and more bizarre. He was oddly fascinated with death, to the point where his friends were worried, and began avoiding him. He often blurt out his thoughts, and while they were comical and socially acceptable when he was a child, they became more bizarre in his teens. He was fond of placing dead crows on his teacher's desk, and when this behavior was not punished, he became increasingly disruptive in class. His grades began to slip, his mind now fully focused on his morbid fascinations. One morning, the teacher found her desk drenched in urine. Despite his classmates maintaining that they had no idea who was responsible, the teacher called in Herb's parents. Herbert Sr. promised that he would have a talk with his son about proper professional behavior. He continued with his classes as usual, and no disciplinary action was taken by the school. By this time, Herb was practically isolated from everyone. His friends were no longer willing to tolerate his strange behavior and bizarre humor, teachers skirted around his issues, his siblings avoided him, and his father found excuses not to be around his son. His mother did care about him, but his personality was so confounding that she broke into tears often when she was around him. By his final year, he was alone and ostracized, and he desperately wanted a new start.

He went on to attend Indiana University, but did not even complete the first semester. Herb's humor and behavior was found contemptible, and he was quickly ostracized and ignored by his classmates. Despite having a wealthy background, he felt like he was treated less than everyone else. He quit before the first semester was out. Herbert Sr. may have had grand plans for his son, but he started to realize that they may not be fulfilled. He pleaded with Herb, asking him to go back to school. When he realized that it was not going to happen, he got his son a job as a copy boy at the Indianapolis Star. His bizarre humor, coupled with his obsession for success and praise, made him the annoying colleague at the office. It soon became clear that he was not meant for the journalistic side, and finally found his place in the advertising side of the company. His twisted sense of humor was enough to keep his colleagues away from him, but the advertising executive, Garry Donna, found it charming and kept making excuses for Herb. His usual phrase was "That is just Herb." However, Herb's attempt at networking with the executives blew up in his face when he showed up with a hearse to take Donna and his close friends to a University of Indiana football game. He became more excluded, the praise he so craved stopped coming in, and he felt that he was not receiving the level of respect he deserved. He became withdrawn and surly, and when he realized that he was never going to be a star at the paper, he quit.

Juliana Saiter

Herbert Sr. was not pleased with how his son's first job had turned out, and was particularly worried about the public shame that Herb had caused the family. He asked Herb to go back to university, and this time he made a deal with his son. If he could finish one single class, he would prove that he was still capable and worthy of help. Herb, completely broken by what transpired at the Indianapolis Star, was more than willing to take up his dad on the offer. He looked at the university's prospectus, and was thrilled when he noted the anatomy class. His morbid fascination with corpses had grown to become an obsession in the past few years, and he was hoping that he would soon get to do an autopsy. Herbert Sr. was happy with his son's choice, and even harbored hope that Herb was following in his father's footsteps.

After he started his classes, it soon became clear that the closest he would come to a dead body was by looking at the pictures in the textbooks. He quickly adjusted, and focused his energy on the class material. He began to excel, and Herbert Sr. was thrilled that his focused and ambitious son was back. As he started excelling, he became quite confident, and was able to find the courage to try and make sense of his sexuality. During his free time, he visited the gay bars and drag acts in Indianapolis. With the clubs full of young men looking to explore, he was lost in the crowd, a quiet man in the corner observing the scene in front of him. His visits became frequent, and he was soon recognized by a number of locals, and they became casual friends. Just as he was about to relax, Herbert Sr. started asking him about his social life, wondering what he did with all the free time after his class. Fearing that he would be found out, he stopped going to the clubs and instead joined the Young Republican's Club at the university. He knew this was something his father would approve of.

Herb's extreme right-wing political views made him a great fit for the club, and since the discussions were serious within the group, he never got the chance to offend anyone with his jokes. His family's wealth and position made him a valued member of the group, and he felt like he was back to his old self. Soon enough, some of the ladies in the group started paying attention to him. Juliana Saiter liked Herb's dressing, and coupled with their mutual interest in cars and shared political views, they seemed like a good match. Herb was quickly to note this, and he found himself faced with a dilemma. Was he going to choose the path he knew his father would approve of or was he going to fulfill his deep seated desires? Herb chose the safer path. He began dating the high school English teacher, stopped frequenting the gay scene, and by all means, seemed like a 'normal' man.

Herb seemed destined for failure, as he failed most of the interviews he attended. He worked at different places for short periods of time, but kept quitting or getting fired. His relationship with Julie was the most stable aspect of his life, and the two quickly got married in November 1971 at the United Methodist Church in Indianapolis. Before they wed, Julie had believed that Herb's strict Christian beliefs was the reason he had not tried to have sex with her. After the marriage, Herb was still not willing to get intimate. He was cold and distant in the bedroom, and he soon started becoming withdrawn. Six months into their marriage, Herbert Sr. came to visit the couple. The next day, Herbert Sr. had his son committed to a mental institution. Julie never asked why. Herb remained at the institution for two months, and he was diagnosed with schizophrenia. Fearing that the community would find out about his son's institutionalization, Herbert Sr. had him discharged. Julie was delighted.

Fox Hollow Farms

After he was released from the institution, Herb started working at the Bureau of Motor Vehicles, a job his father had secured for him. He was calm and collected when he first started out, but over the years, became increasingly hated by his colleagues. He would shout at them and berate them for small mistakes. This was viewed as a great asset by his bosses because Herb's attention to detail made him the highest performer. He pushed his colleagues, and the administration noticed an overall improvement of the company's performance. He was soon on the fast track for a promotion. His personal life, however, was another story. He had been intimate with his wife a few times, but was still drawn to the gay scene. He started taking "walks," or so he told Julie. He made his way to the gay clubs during those "walks" and he became more drawn to the clubs over the years. His visits started getting more and more frequent, and Julie was none the wiser.

In 1979, Herb and Julie had their first child, Marie, with the second, Erich, born two years later. Their last child, Emily, was born five years after the first. Herb was a dedicated father, although time spent with his children meant that he wasn't able to indulge his other passions. Over the years, he started becoming frustrated with his life. His time was spent at work or with his children, and he needed a way to release his pent up frustrations. He began urinating on his boss' desk. Many speculated that Herb was the culprit, but there was never any conclusive evidence. For months, Herb's boss walked into his office to find a piss-soaked desk. When he found the letter from the governor of Indiana soaked in piss, he decided that enough was enough. Herb was given a choice; if he left quietly, his urinating habits would remain a secret. The other option was clear, and Herb accepted his termination without a fuss.

Herbert Sr. visited his son soon after he was fired, and let him know that there were very few jobs available to him. Many in the community had heard rumors about Herb's "practical" joke and were unwilling to hire him. Julie, in a bid to help the family, started teaching part-time to supplement the family income. Herb got various jobs, mainly involving sales that had him traveling away from home for weeks at a time. He finally returned to Indiana and started working as a clerk at a thrift store. He began noting the administration flaws within the store, but his manager was unwilling to implement any. Two years into his job at the store, Herbert Sr. passed away. Herb and Julie helped with the funeral, and soon after began discussing starting their own business. They settled on starting their own thrift store, which Herb had realized had the potential of becoming extremely profitable with the right management. With a $4,000 loan from Herb's mother, they opened the Sav-A-Lot thrift store in 1988 on 46th Street. They made a $50,000 profit in the first year, and soon opened a second location.

As the profits poured in, Herb and Julie mortgaged a new home in 1991. Their new address was Fox Hollow Farms, located in the affluent Westfield District in Hamilton County, 20 miles from Indianapolis. The property featured a Tudor-style mansion and over 18 acres of land.

The Search for Brian Smart

In July 1993, private investigator Virgil Vandagriff got a call from Catherine Araujo, the mother of Roger Goodlet. She explained that her son had been missing for several days, and she had last seen him when he left to go to a gay bar. Goodlet was 32 years old at the time. Araujo had gone to the Indianapolis Police Department to report her son missing, but was told that police would look into it after 30 days had lapsed. She wasn't willing to wait that long. Vandagriff took her case. A few days later, he received a call from the family of Alan Broussard. Broussard was a gay man who had similar features to those of Roger Goodlet, and had last been seen after he went to a gay bar. Vandagriff and his team created missing persons flyers for Goodlet and Broussard, and they began canvassing the local gay bars looking for any information that would help their case. Tips started flowing in, and he soon found out that Goodlet and Broussard were not the only gay men to go missing within the area in the last few years. Multiple callers stated that they had last seen Goodlet entering a blue car with Ohio plates.

Vandagriff and his team staked out various parking lots hoping to see the car with the Ohio plates. They came up empty. When the 30 days lapsed since Broussard's disappearance, the Indianapolis Police

Department also took up the case. They looked into the missing persons records and discovered that since 1992, eight gay men had gone missing. They started looking for a common link, and found out that three of the men had dated the same person. He was soon considered a suspect, and later cleared after police searched his home and found no evidence that he was in any was connected to the disappearances of the eight men. The investigation soon reached a dead end.

Three months after the investigation was launched, Vandagriff received a call that put the case back into the limelight. Tony Harris (a pseudonym created to protect his identity) told Vandagriff that he think he had been with the man responsible for the disappearances of the gay men in the area. Harris was at a club when he struck up a conversation with a white man in his 40s. After they had a few drinks, the man, who identified himself as Brian Smart, invited him back to his place. It was a long drive, and he saw a sign with the word "Farm" as they entered a long winding road before stopping at a mansion. The house was dark, and the man invited him to the pool. They drank some more, and did a little cocaine before swimming in the pool. Smart then convinced him to try erotic asphyxiation, stating that it would be the best orgasm of Harris' life. He asked Harris to step into the pool and then he sat on the edge of the pool behind him. Smart then picked up the swimming pool hose that was lying nearby and put it around Harris' throat. A few moments later, Harris realized that Smart had no intention of releasing the hose. Fearing that he was about to die, he decided to play dead. He heard Smart calling out to him a few times before he finally removed the hose and placed it aside. He lay still for a few moments, and when he opened his eyes, Smart seemed particularly surprised. Harris realized that his missing friends may have gone through the same thing, but had not survived the encounter.

To Vandagriff, the story sounded unbelievable. He called Lieutenant Thom Green, the investigator from the Indianapolis Police Department investigating the cases of the missing gay men. They set up an interview with Harris. They were soon convinced that Harris was telling the truth, and the mystery of how he managed to survive the encounter became clear. Harris stood at 6'5, and the investigators believed that Smart would have tried to kill him again were it not for his body size. A week later, Harris called the investigators, telling them that he had just received a call from Smart asking him to go back to the mansion. The call was traced to a payphone. The investigators asked Harris to call Smart and arrange a meeting at a third location, but Smart never showed. Investigators were desperately looking for any leads, so they went through Harris' statement looking for any leads that were overlooked. They honed in on Harris' statement that Smart had told him he was a caretaker of the house, and that he lived in Ohio. Coupled with statements that Goodlet had been seen in a car with Ohio plates, investigators decided to reach out to officers in Ohio.

The I-70 Murders

The Indianapolis investigators were put in contact with David Lindloff, an investigator with the Preble County Prosecutors Office. Lindloff had a number of missing persons cases going all the way back to 1980. The victims were all young gay men, and the details of their disappearance closely resembled the Indianapolis cases. Lindloff informed Lt. Green that they also had four bodies that had been recovered over the years, in 1985, 1986, 1989, and the last one in 1990. The men had been found dumped on the side of the I-70 highway, naked, or semi-nude. The autopsies had determined that all four men had died of strangulation. The two investigators quickly realized that they may have been looking for the same suspect, and if indeed it was the same killer, then he was the most prolific killer they had ever come across.

Lindloff called the FBI Headquarters and asked for help. They sent five profilers who reviewed the case files and concluded that the killer was in his mid-40s, probably married with kids, and who was afraid of being called gay or being gay.

Search Warrant

As the Indianapolis and Ohio investigations heated up, Vandagriff decided to focus his attention on finding the mansion described by Harris. He and his team pored through various maps, looking for the sign with "Farms" written on it, as well as the long curving driveway. His team drove through different parts of the town looking for the sign. They finally found the property that matched up to the description on East 156th Street: Fox Hollow Farms. Vandagriff sent out one of his best investigators to go check out the property. When he was done, the investigator told Vandagriff that it was definitely the house described by Harris. Vandagriff informed the Indianapolis Police Department about the discovery. Lt. Green quickly noted that the property was out of their jurisdiction, and that they had to contact Hamilton County to get a search warrant. The house belonged to the respected family man and businessman Herbert Baumeister, and the Hamilton County Sheriff's Office refused to believe that Harris' story was true. They declined to offer a search warrant until concrete evidence was presented.

The big break in the case came when Harris once again reached out to the investigators with new information. He stated that he had seen Brian Smart walk into one of the gay bars he was at. Harris hid, and then asked one of his friends to follow the man and note which car he was driving. The friend left through a different door at the same time with Smart, and wrote down the license plate of the car he drove. When investigators ran the plates, they found that it belonged to Herbert Baumeister. They were now convinced that they had their perpetrator. When they investigated Herb's past, they discovered a number of unsettling facts. When Lt. Green spoke to Herb in one of the Sav-A-Lot outlets, he informed him of the murders, and asked if he could search his property. Herb refused.

When the Indianapolis police once again reached out to Hamilton County about the search warrant, the once again refused, and asked that more evidence be provided first.

The Skull in the Yard

When investigators found out that Julie had filed for divorce and that Herb was no longer living at the mansion, they believed that they had finally found a way to search the property. Indianapolis investigators visited Julie at the mansion, and informed her that they were investigating a number of homosexual murders. They stated that Herb was their main suspect, and that they believed the murders had taken place in the house. Julie stated that she had no idea what homosexual murders were, but that she would reach out to her attorney before she made any decision. She called her lawyer, William Wendling, and asked him to find out more about the investigation from the police. Wendling was apprised of the investigation, including the fact that there was a credible witness, car identification, and property identification. Wendling relayed this information back to Julie, and then asked her if she had any information that supported what the investigators were claiming.

She revealed that a few months earlier, Erich had been playing in the yard when he picked up a skeleton and brought it back to the house. When she asked Herb about the skull, he stated that it must have been part of the skeleton that Herbert Sr. had in his practice. He said that the skeleton had been in the garage and that maybe animals may have gotten to it and dragged the bones into the yard. A few days later, she went to where the bones had been and found that they were all gone. She decided not to call the police. Wendling asked her to talk to the police about it but she refuse. She also told him not to say anything to the cops about what she had said.

By June 1996, the divorce proceedings were in full swing. The thrift store business was collapsing, and Herb was desperately fighting to keep the kids. Julie's lawyer, Wendling, was worried that Herb would get desperate enough and hurt Julie or the children. It seemed that this had also occurred to Julie, and on June 24, 1996, she called Wendling and asked him to call the Indianapolis investigators to her house. She had something to say. She took the investigators to the spot where Erich had found the skull. When officers started looking around, one officer pointed out to the bone hidden under some leaves. The investigators finally had enough evidence to secure a search warrant. The Hamilton County Sheriff's Office cooperated fully with the Indianapolis investigators, and crime scene experts were called to the scene.

At the time, Herb was with Eric at his mother's cabin by Lake Wawasee, and had refused to give him back to Julie. Wendling, fearing what Herb would do if the news of the search went public, filed an emergency petition for Herb to hand over Erich back into Julie's custody. Officers from the Hamilton County Sheriff's Office drove up to the cabin and got Erich without incident. No one knows why Herb was not taken into custody at the time. Back at Fox Hollow Farms, the crime scene techs were combing through every inch of the property. Over the course of three days, multiple bones were dug up. As the techs were ready to wind down their search, they found a pile of bones in an area bordering the neighbor's property. Over 5000 bones and bone fragments were recovered, but the skulls were missing. This made identification of the bones virtually impossible. It was later revealed that the bones belonged to 11 different victims.

Despite the mounting evidence, Sergeant Ken Whisman of the Hamilton County Sheriff's Office maintained that the evidence was insufficient to issue an arrest warrant for Herb Baumeister. The Indianapolis investigators were frustrated, but they did not have jurisdiction. They instead focused on building their case against Herb.

Early on the morning of July 4, 1996, Sgt. Whisman received a call from Herb's brother. He revealed that Herb had committed suicide. Canadian authorities had found his car parked on the side of the road, and it was apparent that he had shot himself in the head. This turn of events was a big blow to Lindloff, who strongly believed that Herb was responsible for the I-70 murders.

If true, Herb was responsible for at least 21 murders. His secrets died with him on July 3, 1996.

EVELYN HARTLEY

The scene is a peaceful suburban setting in an area where trouble rarely calls. Excitement fills the air as a big community event ensues, but in one house there is a studious babysitter quietly reading her books while the radio plays softly and the children in their charge sleeps peacefully upstairs. Nothing seems out of the ordinary until the sitter meets a terrifying and untimely end at the hands of a deranged, usually masked, villain. It's become something of a trope in horror movies over the decades, with gargantuan figures, such as Michael Myers from the infamous *Halloween* franchise, preying upon unsuspecting teenagers in unfamiliar locations at the dead of night. But for one teenage girl and her family, this nightmare would become a reality.

Evelyn Grace Hartley was the youngest of four children. Born on November 21, 1937, she lived happily with her family in La Crosse County, Wisconsin. She was an intelligent and caring girl. As a junior at Central High School in 1953, fifteen-year-old Evelyn was an A-grade student who participated in many of the extra-curricular activities the school offered. She had a particular interest in music, was a skilled pianist, and sang in her church's choir every Sunday. Dedicated to her local church, she volunteered as an Officer at the Presbyterian Youth Program and Westminster Fellowship. Evelyn was loving and well-liked, but was known for preferring study over play, favouring a night in with her books over large social events. This was the reason Evelyn accepted a babysitting job at 2415 Hoeschler Drive on Saturday October 24, 1953.

Viggo Rasmusen worked with Evelyn's father, Richard Hartley, as a professor at La Crosse State College. He was in need of a stand-in babysitter for that particular Saturday evening in October, as his usual sitter, Janice Lucille Cowley, had plans to attend the homecoming game at the school the same evening. Rasmusen also wanted to attend the event to cheer on his La Crosse State College students as they faced their competitors, River Falls. Knowing Evelyn to be a responsible girl in Cowley's class at school, Viggo approached Richard with the idea that Evelyn look after his twenty-month-old daughter, also named Janice. Richard discussed the idea with his daughter, and true to her reliable and responsible nature, Evelyn accepted. Before being picked up by Viggo at 6.30pm, she packed a bag with a variety of school books, planning to study while the baby slept, and promised her father that she would call at 8.30pm to let him know everything was going well. But the phone did not ring at the Hartley residence that night.

Richard Hartley began to worry as 8.30pm passed with no news from his daughter. It was out of character for Evelyn to break her word. Richard tried calling the Rasmusen house several times to no avail. At 9.20pm, he decided to drive to the house and check in on his daughter in person. There was no answer when he arrived and rang the doorbell, causing him further concern. All of the lights appeared to be on in the house and he could hear the faint sound of the radio playing, yet there was no sound of movement. Making his way around the outside of the house, he found all of the doors were locked. Eventually able to enter the building, he was confronted with every parent's worst nightmare: the scene of a violent struggle.

The Rasmusen's living room was in disarray, with the furniture upturned and moved to different parts of the room. Evelyn's school books were scattered across the floor. Her eyeglasses and one of her shoes were laying discarded in the living room, alongside footprints from a pair of sneakers. Panicked, Richard searched the house to try and find his daughter. He found various household items strewn around the home. Checking the baby's room, Richard saw that Janice lay asleep in her crib, but there was no sign of Evelyn anywhere in the house. Pry marks were found at three of the home's windows, but all entry points to the newly developed home were locked and secure, except from the basement at the back of the house. Making his descent into the lower part of the house, Richard found Evelyn's other shoe. He then discovered an open window in the basement with the screen missing, later to be discovered leaning against an outside wall. Another set of footprints made by sneakers were visible in the window box. Positioned by the open window was a small stepladder the Rasmusens had been using while painting their new home, and on the floor was a horrifying pool of blood. The blood trail continued outside, with two large pools found in the yard, further blood stains on the walls of a neighbour's house, and a bloody handprint approximately four feet off of the ground on a garage wall just down the street from the Rasmusen home.

At approximately 9.49pm, Richard rushed across the street to Frank Linder's home and urged him to call the police. Authorities quickly arrived on the scene and began their investigation. Finding footprints similar to those in and around the Rasmusen home in various areas around the neighbourhood, police suggested that the kidnapping wasn't predetermined, although there is debate as to whether or not the attacker saw Evelyn enter the house. A botched robbery was also discounted as a motive, as nothing of value was taken from the home. The police determined that the attacker must have carried Evelyn across the yard, putting her down at the two scenes where blood had collected. Aghast at the sight of these blood pools, Evelyn's mother, Ethel, was reportedly convinced that her daughter was dead at the scene of the crime. However, investigating officers speculated that the blood wasn't an indicator of fatal injuries, instead suspecting that it may have been caused by a bloody nose. They used bloodhounds to track Evelyn's scent, following a trail that led for two blocks, stopping at Coulee Drive, With the trail ending so suddenly, the authorities believed that she was likely placed in a vehicle and driven away. This theory was reiterated by information from local man, Ed Hofer. On October 26, Hofer approached the authorities, stating his vehicle was nearly hit by a speeding two-tone green Buick at roughly 7.15pm on the night of the incident. He saw three figures in the car: one male in the driver's seat, another male in in back, and a girl, slumped forward with her head against the front seat's headrest. Initially assuming the trio were heading to the homecoming game, Hofer didn't think anything of it, and left the Buick to continue its drive westward. It wasn't until he heard the news of Evelyn's disappearance the next day that he realised the significance of what he had witnessed.

As locals continued to come forward with information, the homecoming game would prove to have repeatedly prevented Evelyn's chances of receiving help from anyone nearby. Nearby neighbours, Elvin and Helen Saterback, told the police they had heard two or three concerning screams at approximately 7pm, with the final scream sounding as if it had been cut short. The witnesses assumed the noise was just rowdy children carried away by the excitement of the game, and the abrupt end to the last cry had been caused by the child being taken indoors to be scolded by parents. Helen admitted she thought the screaming sounded like cries telling someone to "stop" or "get away". Similarly, a passer-by told the police that he had witnessed two young men dragging an apparently dazed young female along, but once again assumed it was just youngsters who had been carried away by the celebrations, drinking too much. The collective evidence allowed police to deduce that Evelyn had been abducted at approximately 7pm, meaning the incident happened early into her babysitting shift, as the Rasmusens had left for the game at 6.45pm. Further bad news was delivered to the police as the FBI informed John Bosshard, the La Cross County District Attorney, that they would not get involved in the case, claiming the initial evidence presented did not suggest the crime scene was one of a federal offense, ultimately deeming it a sex crime rather than kidnap or murder.

While the FBI rebuffed Evelyn and the Hartley family, La Crosse County saw the biggest search party in the state of Wisconsin continue to grow. Regular radio bulletins were aired, urging people to volunteer their time to look for the missing girl. As word spread, locals rushed to the area offering to help. It was estimated that at least 1,000 people joined the search within the first 24 hours, including representatives from the Naval Reserve, the Army Reserve, the Auxiliary Police Force, Wisconsin's National Guard, and Boy Scouts, as well as staff and students from La Crosse State College where Richard Hartley and Viggo Rasmusen worked. The nearby rivers were routinely dragged, and the Civil Air Patrol searched from the air, regularly volunteering their resources to the search, flying from Winona, Minnesota, to Stoddard, Wisconsin, while the Air Force also deployed helicopters to scan the area. Hunters were asked to keep an eye open while trekking the woods. Evelyn's brother, Thomas, repeatedly drove the family car along nearby highways in hope of finding some trace of his sister. The community raised funds to enable the Hartley family to offer a reward for any information, amounting to an impressive total of $6,600, which would be just under $61,000 today. The *La Crosse Tribune* reported on October 26, "Saturday night was a sleepless one for the girl's parents ... their family as well as the Rasmusens. It didn't matter to the Rasmusens that thousands trampled their recently sodded lawn around the beautiful new home. They knew the majority of the folks had come out to lend a friendly hand." Indeed, the La Crosse County police department were criticised for allowing so many citizens into the crime scene so soon after the event, fearing evidence may have been tampered with. Nevertheless, people continued to help, and the police remained very open with their investigation.

A few days later, the police uncovered a pair of pants and a brassiere lying at the side of the road near the underpass on Highway 14, just two miles south of Evelyn's home town. Four miles further along the highway, a bloodstained pair of men's pants were found. Whether the three items of clothing were connected remains inconclusive, but the blood on the clothing matched Evelyn's blood type. Soon after, on November 19, the police followed a lead having been tipped off by various farmers. They had each driven past the same peculiar items in the Coon Valley area to the southeast of La Crosse, and reported them to the police. Lying by the side of the road was a pair of size eleven Goodrich sneakers, and just 800 feet away from the shoes was a tired size 36 denim jacket, covered in blood on the front, back, and sleeves. Once again, the blood matched Evelyn's type. Authorities were encouraged by this discovery, considering the shoes to be "the most important pieces of evidence we have in the abduction of fifteen-year-old Evelyn Hartley." The police believed the shoes had been abandoned at the side of the highway shortly before they were found, perhaps as a distraction technique. Upon closer inspection of the items, police discovered the sneakers' soles had a suction-cup pattern which closely matched the footprints at the crime scene. There was also a distinctive wear pattern on the soles which led experts to conclude that the owner regularly rode a Whizzer motorbike. Reaching out to the Goodrich company, they were able to determine the name of the particular style of shoe, "Hood Mogul", and the states they were sold in, helping to narrow the search. Furthermore, each of these shoes had a serial number, which the police used in attempt to trace the owner. However, it was possible the shoes were second hand. This make of shoe hadn't been sold in the Wisconsin area for nearly three years, and experts suggested that two different people had worn the shoes, being too small for the second wearer. The jacket also had distinctive features, with metallic buttons and a strip cut from the bottom and roughly re-hemmed. A well-worn print into the fabric of the jacket suggested that the owner of the clothing may have worked as a steeplejack. Certain these items had been worn by Evelyn's abductor, the police travelled to 31 different communities in the Wisconsin area, showing the shoes and jackets to the public. Although more than 10,000 people were exposed to these pieces of evidence, no one recognised them, proving to be a devastating blow to the one promising lead authorities had uncovered.

Thorough investigations continued throughout La Crosse County's surrounding community. A sticker campaign was launched on October 29th. Police Chief George Long was intent on searching all of the cars in the county, and ordered gas station attendants to check vehicles for bloodstains. Searched cars which turned no evidence were given a sticker which read "My Car is OK". Over 40,000 of these stickers were printed. Any drivers who refused the inspection had to be reported to the police. Fresh graves were even reopened to ensure Evelyn's remains had not been hidden alongside a recent burial. With few clues coming to light, authorities took drastic measures and began conducting mass polygraphing, intending to test all the high school boys in the area to see if they knew anything about the disappearance. The *La Crosse Tribune* stated that the police were able to test four boys within an hour on the first day of testing, asking just five simple questions to each interviewee. Unfortunately, the testing proved too controversial within the community, and was halted after only 300 participants had cleared the polygraph.

It has been estimated that during the first year of Evelyn's disappearance, over 2,000 people helped in the search, making it the largest ever of its kind in Wisconsin. Police claim that during that same time period, they questioned over 3,500 people in connection with the disappearance. Unfortunately, their diligent searching turned no leads, leaving the Hartley family heartbroken and hopeless. Her father openly appealed for information regularly, urging the abductor to come forward, "I know that the police department and the other authorities are doing everything possible with the meagre information they have to find Evelyn or her abductor ... Of course, the person who has the most information is the abductor. I am appealing to him to reveal the location of Evelyn or her body. I do not expect him to reveal his identity. But he can give us something to lead us to the girl."

The authorities received many dead-end leads and false confessions following Evelyn's abduction. Shortly after the news of Evelyn's disappearance broke, a woman in Madison, Wisconsin, requested that police arrest her fifteen-year-old son in relation to the case. The boy had run away from his home in May 1953, returned home for a few days, and left again on October 24th. He reappeared in early November to collect some of his clothing and possessions, where he told his mother that he knew Evelyn and had dated her. Upon receiving this tip, police rushed from La Crosse County to Madison to take the boy in for questioning, but were ultimately left with little evidence that he had been involved in the case. In fact, Richard Hartley was insistent that he had never met the boy, and the family's relationship was so open that he would have been aware of any boyfriends Evelyn might have had. Although she had been on a few dates, she had never been courted by a boy long-term. A local man named Jack Duffrin also claimed to have information about the case. The twenty-year-old called the Hartley family twice in response to their public appeals for information. Each time, he offered to exchange key information in return for $500. Working together, the Hartleys and the authorities set up a trap for Duffrin and caught both the suspect and a thirteen-year-old boy. Proving to have no real knowledge about the case, Duffrin was ultimately arrested, convicted, and imprisoned for extortion.

The police also closely interrogated recently arrested criminals in hopes of gaining any clues. It was estimated that seventy-five sex offenders were questioned and cleared of involvement. Forty-three-year-old Bernard J Lauer was held on a rape charge shortly after the incident. The salesman, originally from Eau Claire, was in the area selling roofing in late October 1953, but he had a reliable alibi for the night of Evelyn's disappearance. A twenty-year-old man, Robert Snodgrass, was questioned in the days following the abduction. He had been arrested for indecent exposure, but his alibi for the evening was also solid. Another young man, John Mulqueen, was arrested after confessing to the murder of an army captain near Menomonie. Once again, there was no evidence to link Mulqueen to Evelyn's abduction, and upon tracing activity on his gasoline credit card, it was revealed he was in Houston on October 24th. Hayverd Tygue became another suspect in the case. The nineteen-year old had been arrested for driving a stolen car from his home city of Chicago to Wisconsin. As he was questioned, details of further crimes became apparent, bearing striking similarities to Evelyn's case. Tygue had attacked two women in Madison. In one instance, he broke into a house in a newly developed neighbourhood by entering through the basement window. He attacked his unsuspecting victims with a baton, but fled each time when the women began screaming. Police searched the car in question, a tan colour vehicle with Illinois license plates. It appeared to match the description a neighbour provided of a car circling the neighbourhood three times at roughly 8pm the evening before Evelyn was taken. The police also found a lead pipe with human hairs on it in the vehicle. Tygue was ultimately questioned, but once again lead to a dead-end for police, as he was not in La Crosse on the night of October 24th.

Perhaps the most notorious criminal linked to the case was Ed Gein. Known as the Butcher of Plain Field, Gein was a murderer and body snatcher who used his victim's skin and bones to make stomach-churning trophies which police found in his house. His disturbed mind has been forever immortalized in fiction and popular culture, influencing the creation of characters such as Norman Bates in Robert Bloch's novel and Alfred Hitchcock's silver screen adaptation, *Psycho*, and Leatherface in movie franchise, *The Texas Chainsaw Massacre*. Following his arrest, it was discovered that he was in La Crosse County at the time of Evelyn's disappearance, and he happened to be visiting a relative who lived just a few blocks away from the Rasmusen residence. Denying any involvement, Gein took two lie detector tests in relation to Evelyn's case, but passed them both. Police searched Gein's house of horrors for any evidence, but found nothing that suggested Evelyn had fallen victim to Gein. In November 1957, Gein was publicly cleared of any involvement in the case. Considered legally insane, Gein spent the rest of his life in a mental institution. His involvement in the case is still debated today, as his presence in La Crosse during the time of the disappearance seems too coincidental to some, while his unstable mental state could potentially make his testimony and any test results unreliable. However, it would also have been out of character for Gein to work with an accomplice, and it seems unlikely that he would have broken his pattern of keeping trophies.

The case gained such notoriety in the area, that people continued to provide false confessions decades after the event. In 1971, a fifty-one-year-old transient man named Tommy Thompson was arrested in Casper, Wyoming for cashing bad checks. During his questioning, he claimed that he had kidnapped, raped, and murdered a fifteen-year-old babysitter in La Crosse County in 1953. Police investigated further, but found Thompson was serving time in a Minnesota prison during the time of the abduction. Instead, he was charged for making a false statement. Further evidence was revealed in 2004, when police finally hoped they had caught the break they were looking for, fifty years after Evelyn went missing. While researching a book about the case, Andy Thompson, Peggy Lovejoy, and Susan T. Hessel's investigation triggered a memory for Wisconsin man, Mel Williams. In 1968, Williams was recording in The Raven, a bar in La Forge. At the time, he was a musician and would regularly tape bands playing. A visitor to the area, Williams wanted to get some of the local characters on tape, and was drawn to one man in particular, telling the *La Crosse Tribune* in 2004, "This (man) was quite a character, buying booze for a bunch of alcoholic friends. I wanted him on tape for the memory." The character turned out to be Clyde Tywee Peterson, and he was standing at the bar with a man named Whitey Barclay. In the recording, the pair clearly allude to Evelyn's abduction. In the released transcription, Barclay can be heard to say, "That's ... about the time you hauled that Hartley girl down there ... That right?" The men continued to discuss the disappearance, referring to the police searching graves and repeatedly naming the Hartley family, with Barclay going so far as to say, "You know damn right he all done it ... and I know it, and he told me with his own mouth." In the recording, they implicate a man named Jack Gaulthair, and reveal that his role in the abduction drove him to suicide. Indeed, it was publicly reported that Gaulthair had taken his own life on Christmas Day, 1967. The recording ends with Barclay stating his theories on where Evelyn's body might be buried and mentioning another unnamed man who might know what really happened to her, before turning to Williams and demanding he stop the tape, "shut it off, shut it off!" The County Sheriff in place in 2004 was Gene Carey, who agreed that this discovery could prove vital to the case. Unfortunately, being so many years after the recording was made, this new lead failed to open any new doors.

Sixty-five years later, the tragic disappearance of Evelyn Hartley still remains unsolved. Her parents eventually moved to Oregon to be close to their daughter, Carolyn, ultimately accepting that it was unlikely their youngest child would ever be found. The abductor remains unmasked, and the case continued to haunt the Rasmusen family, who moved to a new home soon after Evelyn's abduction. Speaking with the La Crosse Tribune on the twenty-fifth anniversary of the event, Viggo Rasmusen stated the whole experience continued to be "a nightmare, whenever we think of it. I don't mean it preys on our minds constantly, but we don't forget it no matter how long ago it was." Their daughter, Janice, grew up with a detailed knowledge of the case, but no memory of the events. As an active baby, her parents were always thankful that she slept quietly and peacefully on the night of October 24th, not alerting the criminal to her presence in the house. The disappearance demonstrated the true power of community. The vast number of volunteers and the generous donations locals made to the case was astounding. Even four years after her abduction, 84-year-old Howard George spent the little money he had to hire private investigators from the Hargrave Secret Services for three months to help with the case. Unfortunately, by the time they had completed their report, they had compiled no new evidence or leads, and Howard had passed away. In a devastating case haunted by continuous dead-ends, false confessions, and no closure, lies the heart of a dedicated community committed to ensuring Evelyn's memory lives on.

finding jodi

CHRISSY THOMPSON

Jodi Sue Huisentruit was a news anchor for KIMT, a station based in Mason City, Iowa. On June 27th, 1995, she called the station and told her co-worker that she was on her way to work after she overslept.

It would be the last time anyone heard from her.

There were signs of a struggle outside of her apartment indicating that she had been abducted. She would disappear without a trace. Numerous rumors and "persons of interest" have emerged but no official suspect has ever been named.

Over twenty years later, the question still remains.

What happened to Jodi Huisentruit?

EARLY LIFE

Jodi was born in Long Prairie, Minnesota, the youngest daughter of Maurice Huisentruit and Imogene "Jane" Huisentruit. Her father would pass away at age sixty-two of colon cancer. Jodi was only fourteen at the time.

Jodi was an excellent student who also excelled at golf. She would lead her high school team to victory in the state Class A tournament in 1985 and 1986. After high school, she would attend St. Cloud State University where she majored in TV Broadcasting and Speech Communication.

After graduating college, she worked for Northwest Airlines as a stewardess until she landed her first broadcasting gig at KGAN in Cedar Rapids, Iowa. She then briefly returned to Minnesota to work at KSAX before relocating to Iowa for a job at KIMT.

Jodi was well-liked at the station and immediately became a hit with her viewers who liked the infectious enthusiasm of the sunny blonde. She was petite, blonde and had a made for television smile.

Family members, however, would often worry about Jodi as they perceived her as a bit naïve.

"She would befriend anyone," investigative reporter Steve Powell said. "It was part of her nature and that is what made her a popular fixture at the station. In some of her family home videos, you can see the playfulness of her nature. She was outgoing and bubbly. Not the type of person who made enemies."

"I hired Jodi," said Doug Merbach, former news director of KIMT. "I brought her to Mason City. Could there have been something we could have warned her about and talked to her about? I don't know. What do you think happened? I've been asked that so many times. I feel as ignorant as the next person. I just don't know. I don't want to point fingers at anybody without looking inside the investigation and opening up those books. I don't know. I think it had to be somebody who knew her. I think it had to be somebody who had an emotional response to something Jodi said or did that caused them to do that. I don't think it was random - I don't think it was planned. I think it was planned to a certain extent - but not days and weeks ahead of time."

"She had so much enthusiasm," her best friend at the station, Robin Woflram said. "Every day was a gift and treated as something to explore. Sometimes occasionally she would call, I mean this girl got up at 3 am, and she said 'What are you doing after work?' It's like 10:30 pm and I'd tell her that I'm going home and going to bed. She'd say, 'Oh, Robin, there's plenty of time to sleep. Life is for the living.' And she embraced every single moment."

"It's sometimes difficult to get close - especially women - in this industry because you're always looking over your shoulder and wondering if someone is coming up behind me. I'll never forget the first day she walked in and her laugh. She'll always be remembered for that. She's fun and spunky. I think I'll like her. She's got zest for living."

JODI IS MISSING

Huisentruit would play in a golf tournament the day before she disappeared. She then went to the home of John Vansice and according to him, they watched a videotape of her birthday party that he had arranged for her.

On June 27th, 1995, KIMT producer Amy Kuns noticed that Jodi still had not reported for work. She called her at the apartment and explained that she had overslept.

"I'm on my way," Jodi said.

Two hours later, Jodi still had not arrived at the station.

Kuns would substitute for her on her morning show Daybreak.

An hour later, she would call the Mason City police.

"It became known only after that Jodi wasn't always punctual," Powell said. "A lot of her co-workers covered for her because they didn't want her to get in trouble with the brass at the station. So, her arriving late wasn't that much of an unusual occurrence. Not showing up at all certainly was, however, and they called for the police to do a welfare check."

Police would arrive at Jodi's apartment and find her red Mazda Miata still parked in the apartment lot. There was evidence suggesting that there had been a struggle near her car.

Jodi's keys were stuck in the driver side door, broken in half. Her blow dryer, jewelry, and red high heels were strewn about in the parking lot.

The top of her convertible was dented. Blood and tissue was splattered on the driver side mirror. Skid marks on the pavement suggested that she had been dragged to a waiting vehicle."

"The scene suggested that she had been grabbed while putting her keys in the car door," Powell said. "She was in a rush, having overslept for whatever reason. Was probably going to make herself up on the way to the station when someone rushed up behind her."

There was a palm print left behind on her car which police were never able to identify.

MORNING SCREAMS

Police would inquire with neighbors and found three tenants who stated that they heard screams in the early morning hours. Another neighbor reported seeing a white van with lights on parked nearby Jodi's vehicle.

Three months after her disappearance, Jodi's family would hire private investigators from McCarthy and Associates (MAIS) in Minneapolis who then worked in tandem with another private investigator, Doug Jasa.

"A lot of things struck me about the case," Jasa said. "I still remember all of the cards they found in Jodi's apartment. They were birthday cards. I think there were 50 of them and we're reading through them - reading through them. People had written very nice notes in the birthday cards. We went door to door in the apartment complex - talking with different residences about what they heard. One lady remembers specifically looking at her clock when she heard the scream."

Her family held out hope throughout the harrowing ordeal.

"I couldn't have had a better kid sister," Jodi's older sister Joanne Nathe said. "She tried to motivate me. What are your goals? That makes me stronger. It's a nightmare...not knowing where she is. We were hoping to find her in the first few months."

Neither the police nor the private investigators would come up with any evidence. All they had were more questions.

Questions that would forever remain unanswered.

"What caused her to sleep in that day," Officer Terrance Prochaska with Mason City Police Department asked. "What caused her to answer the phone and rush into work? What was she doing the night before? We all want to know the fine details. We know where she was at. She was golfing. She had driven home and made a phone call to her friend. Those are facts. But its' that gray area in between that we don't understand."

Rumors would plague the investigation as numerous false hopes and bizarre allegations were made. Mason City had a growing drug problem and some speculated that Jodi was working on a story to expose drug dealers. This was an outlandish claim considering that Jodi was not an investigative reporter and was not trained for that discipline. KIMT was a call-in television station. They got their news from the wires and reported it after some fact-checking. Another unfounded rumor came from a disgruntled female police officer who claimed that two of her fellow officers were responsible for Jodi's disappearance. Again, these were uncorroborated allegations and the officer spreading the rumors was terminated.

The community at large would get involved and in May of 1996, over one hundred volunteers searched the area of Cerro Gordo County. They would leave flags in the ground to mark anything they found to be suspicious. Authorities would then comb through the area but no further evidence was ever found.

Over one thousand interviews were conducted after her disappearance. Not one single suspect ever emerged.

Police initially turned their attention to the last person to have seen Jodi alive.

John Vansice.

Vansice was a lifelong Iowa native and lived in Newton where he was married with two children. He divorced in the early 1990s and moved to the Key Apartments in Mason City where he would befriend Jodi.

Jodi would reportedly spend a lot of time with the fifty-year-old Vansice. He was more than twenty years her senior and seemed to be "obsessed" with her. He threw around more money than his listed occupation (corn seeder) would suggest he could afford as he purchased a $26,000 boat in 1995 which he named "Jodi".

Jodi's purchase of the Mazda Miata seemed fishy as well as the car was more expensive than her meager salary as a broadcaster would allow.

STRANGER OR STALKER?

"I was the last to see her alive," Vansice said as he approached law enforcement officers investigating Jodi's apartment. He told police of what happened the night before, that Jodi was at his apartment watching a birthday video.

Vansice had taken special care in throwing Jodi a birthday party. He had printed out the invites himself, making sure his name was printed on the bottom with the words "a party given by John Vansice and friends."

Joann described Vansice as being "fixated" on her sister but stated that Jodi never mentioned anything about him during their conversations. She did mention Vansice in conversations with her mother and alluded to the fact that he may be developing a romantic interest in her. She also stated that she felt "uncomfortable" during a recent breakfast she had with Vansice.

Joann would describe a meeting she had with Vansice in which she thought his behavior was "cold" and "unfriendly." She asked Vansice if Jodi ever mentioned their Dad to him and he abruptly ended their conversation.

During his public appearances, Vansice seemed calm in relaying his support for Jodi's return.

Too calm.

"We're all praying and hoping that she's okay," Vansice said. "We just have to keep praying and keep hoping and I'll think she'll come back. I really do."

"I liked Jodi so much I named my boat after her," Vansice said when asked by a reporter why he named his boat after her. "She was such a big part of my life and she just made me feel so good."

Jodi's friend, Tammy Baker, once asked Jodi point blank if she was involved with Vansice.

"Absolutely not," Jodi said.

"Vansice was questioned by police but ruled out as he passed the lie detector tests," Powell said. "But any sociopath can pass a lie detector test. Vansice should have been suspect number one on the basis of telling the police that he 'was the last one to see her alive.' Making a statement like that, with no dead body found, is a revealing disclosure."

Most people close to the case believe that Vansice is involved but never directly say his name as if they are afraid.

"It is a head scratcher as to why the police didn't come at him harder," Powell said. "It was almost as if there was a veil of secrecy over his relationship with Jodi and what it exactly entailed. I believe that it may have been in part to protect Jodi's reputation. She was an All-American girl, church-raised and church-going. But the question had to be asked of what her relationship with Vansice exactly was or more specifically, what did he have in mind? Did he want to be her older sugar daddy? He bought her gifts, gave her birthday parties, making deposits in the account so to speak. But when he finally came to collect did she rebuff his advances and spur him to murderous anger?"

"What is certain is that he was her neighbor and they would hang out a lot. When they looked into her apartment they would find four cans of sixteen-ounce beers. No way the petite Jodi could handle that and then head off to work. The toilet seat was up. The other thing missing from her apartment was her personal notebook. Most sexual predators wouldn't steal something like that. But again, hindsight is 20/20 and they should have made a beeline for Vansice's boat the moment they found out that he named his boat after a woman whom he supposedly had a platonic relationship with."

THE DEATH OF A FRIEND

Three months prior to her disappearance, Jodi suffered the loss of a close friend named Billy Pruin. Pruin had just proposed to his girlfriend Gretchen Tusler and two days later he drove to Mason City to pick up a new tractor he had purchased. The next day, a friend went to his farmhouse and saw that his front door was ajar with the keys in the outside lock. He called out for his friend, received no answer, then he left.

No one had heard from Billy and then his mother went to his house to check on him. She would find him laying in a pool of blood, he had been shot in the chest.

Investigators listed his death as a suicide but later changed it to "undetermined".

His friends, Jodi included, could not believe that the jovial Billy committed suicide. He had just proposed to his girlfriend and bought a new tractor for a business. He had no reason to kill himself.

When Jodi disappeared, there was conjecture that the two deaths could be related.

His fiancee, Gretchen, was questioned after his death and stated that he often appeared "afraid of something" for weeks before his death.

Jodi voiced the same concerns prior to her disappearance. She written one of her best friends, Kelly Torgelson, revealing that "she was concerned for her safety, that she was being stalked."

Kelly would receive Jodi's letter in the mail on June 27th, 1995 at her home in Mississippi. The day that Jodi would be abducted.

"Jodi had reported that that a man in a pickup truck stopped and eyeballed her," Powell said. "This creeped her out. She felt as if someone was after her. So that is another theory that we have to go on in the case. Because of her position in the media and being a very attractive female, she was prone to have any nut ball start to fantasize and stalk her."

NO BODY, NO EVIDENCE

The investigators continued to grasp at straws while not pursuing anything against Vansice. They simply had nothing to pin him with.

Desperate for answers, the detectives and members of Jodi's family would meet with psychics in November of 1997.

"Psychics would be called upon a lot during the 1980s and 1990s," Powell said. "It was simply a sign of desperation from everyone involved. They needed anything, just anybody with some type of answer. So these charlatans would come in and they would go through the motions. When that happens, you know that the investigators have absolutely nothing."

Jodi's disappearance would leave her co-workers at KIMT devastated. Some left the business while others moved to other stations. Not one colleague that worked with Jodi during her tenure at KIMT remains with the station.

Wolfram, Jodi's friend and fellow broadcaster, would leave KIMT a few months after Jodi disappeared.

"They called me into the office and I thought they had found Jodi," Wolfram recalled. "Otherwise, why would all these people be in the office than to share that information. But there was talk on the internet - chat rooms - he claimed he knew who had abducted Jodi. Gruesome details. Then the reason they had brought me in was the last communication was that Robin Wolfram would be next. From that point on - I had a police escort at night. From that point forward, I look at life differently. I think I used to look at life in rose colored glasses and everyone had a pure heart like Jodi. I realized evil exists right next door to good. It's like a veil. You reach your hand across to experience it. And it's not that easy."

NEW LEADS, MORE FALSE HOPES

Jodi's case would remain in the public eye and garnered renewed interest on the 20th year anniversary of her disappearance.

In a bizarre twist, photocopies of Jodi's personal diary were anonymously mailed to a local newspaper in June of 2008. The journal was eighty-four pages long and sent to the Mason City Globe Gazette. The diary had been placed in a large envelope with no return address. Days later, however, the sender had come forward.

It was the wife of the former Mason City Police Chief.

Her motive for sending the copy to the newspaper remains unclear.

JODI'S JOURNAL

Jodi would start "journaling" after she purchased Anthony Robbins Success program.

Her entries would reveal some of her personal thoughts and how she prioritized things in terms of work, family, and friends. Throughout the pages, she expressed her love for travel, socializing and her search for someone to share her life with.

"Remember," one of her first entries read, "there is no time better than now to begin practicing being the best I can be and living the way I want to live."

Jodi would continue to write about her goals and desire to get the "Huisentruit name out." She listed Paula Zahn and Kathy Gifford as her role models.

She wrote about her dating life briefly, talking about male friends and her love for dancing. She had met a man she liked during a cruise she had taken with her mother. "Why do I get hooked so fast?" she asked in one entry. "I'm lonely here at times and would like to have someone to share my life with. Sure I meet men — but none that really strikes me, or who follows thru."

"My No. 1 goal is to get a new job," she wrote in April 1995, two months before her disappearance.

"I'm recovering from Memorial Day Weekend, unbelievable — Indy 500 — a time of my life. Partied with so many wonderful people — Mario Andretti (world class racer), Joe Dumars (Detroit Pistons basketball player) and Tim Allen (TV star from 'Home Improvement'). Had an incredible weekend."

The latter part of her entries focused more on her activities as opposed to her goals.

"I stayed in Mason City this weekend to regroup, gather my thoughts and goals, read! And have Jodi time. I've enjoyed it. Church is very important to me as is putting myself and family ... at the top. I'm starting fresh at work this week — getting up at 3 a.m. — best newscast in the world — top 10 market — I really think I'll market myself for AZ. — see what they think about my accent. Or I'll move down there to produce."

Her final three entries all mention John Vansice.

"What a weekend, Surprise," Jodi wrote on June 11, 1995. "My Mason City/Clear Lake friends thru a big party for me! At a lounge, wild. It was in Clear Lake. They had a 16 gal keg – huge cake (with a skier) so much left. John Van Sice grilled 150 pork burgers, we were dancing on tables...dancing everywhere...Everyone had a ball. Video camera was rolling, cameras were clicking – oh what fun! Life is so good. The party made me feel so good."

"Last night John,...and I went to the Glen Miller Orchestra in Belmond," Jodi wrote on June 13th, 1995. "I have so many great viewers. People are so kind. This nice weather has me wild. I bought a new Mazda Miata, simply love it."

"Got home from a weekend road trip to Iowa City," Jodi wrote in her final entry. "oh we had fun! It was wild, partying and water skiing. We skied at the Coralville Res. I'm improving on the skis — hips up, lean, etc. John's son Trent gave me some great ski tip advice. Today, Sunday, it was raining in Mason City so didn't get any skiing in. I love it, it's addicting." Later on in the entry she wrote about her desire to move on from KIMT. "Great friends but professionally, I'm fed up. It's difficult finding a new job and I'm confused about agent and what to do."

The journals didn't reveal any clues that furthered the investigation. It remains a head-scratcher as to why the wife of the former police chief would forward the journal to the newspaper.

"The journals said a lot about Jodi's character," Powell said. "Reading through it is heartbreaking because you realize how much she loved her life, her family, and friends. She was on the road to self-improvement and listened to Tony Robbins' success tapes. She aspired to beyond what she was doing. She wanted to make her mark."

NEW SUSPECT

One new suspect that did emerge in recent years was serial rapist Tony Dejuan Jackson. Jackson was twenty-one years old at the time of Huisentruit's abduction and is now serving a life sentence in Minnesota for raping three women in 1997.

He was questioned about the crime and denied ever meeting Huisentruit or seeing her in public.

His former friend, however, stated otherwise.

Speaking anonymously, this friend would tell the Minneapolis news station KMSP that he had met Jackson because their girlfriends at the time were good friends. The source described an occasion where Jackson had invited him to get drinks where he knew Jodi was a regular.

The two then arrived at the South Bridge Lounge where they saw Jodi sitting at the bar.

He stated that Jackson walked right up to Jodi and began talking to her but he didn't hear the gist of their conversation.

Jackson was living in Mason City at the time and was attending North Iowa Community College. He hosted his own student talk show and wanted to pursue a career in broadcasting.

His friend thought that Jackson simply wanted to get career advice from Jodi not really thinking anything of their conversation until years later.

"My gut tells me that he probably did it," Jackson's friend said. "After all the stuff he's done since."

This suspicion of Jackson is corroborated with a neighbor who went out jogging early in the morning. She stated that the morning before she saw a young African American man, riding a bike outside the complex. He started biking ride beside her and she was spooked by him as it was so early in the morning.

Jackson would eventually be connected to over six sexual assaults on women from North Iowa to the St. Paul area in Minnesota.

He would arm himself with handcuffs, duct tape, mask and a gun as he stalked his victims. He threatened to kill his victims when they would not submit to him. One of his victims was eventually able to identify him as she worked with Jackson at a restaurant.

Jackson would write rap songs in prison that contained the lyric "stiffin' around Tiffin." Authorities believed that he may be referring to a silo in Tiffin, Iowa which he may have dumped her body. He had also told a cellmate that he was involved with a kidnapping of a news anchor.

Mason City police would not charge him, however, and it remains unclear why the eliminated him as a suspect.

As of this writing, John Vansice remains the primary person of interest. He has since moved to Phoenix, Arizona.

Jodi would be declared legally dead in May of 2001.

THE DISAPPEARANCE OF BRITTANEE DREXEL

FAITH TORINO

Brittanee Drexel disappeared from Myrtle Beach, SC while on spring break on April 25, 2009. She was 17 at the time and traveled without receiving parental consent. She told her mother that she was staying at a friend's house near their home in Rochester, New York. Brittanee's mother, Dawn, then learned where she really was when her boyfriend, John, called her after he suspected something had happened to Brittanee. Her parents immediately grew angry, scared, and devastated when they received word that their daughter was missing.

Brittanee was born on October 7th, 1991 and lived in Rochester, New York. She moved frequently during her youth as her father was in the military. She was a junior at Gates-Chili High school and the year was a rough one with her parents separating. She would live with her mother but still see her father frequently.

She was blind in her right eye and had several surgeries to correct her hyperplastic primary vitreous. To keep her eye from wandering, she would get contacts that made both eyes look the same.

Britt was described by friends and family as a smiling, fun-loving girl. Her demeanor had changed by her junior year in high school as she was depressed that her parents were separating. She would sleep in late and begin to skip school. She would overdose two times on her mother's pain medication and both times were fueled by the fact that she had just broken up with her on-again, off-again boyfriend, John Grieco.

"I felt it was all my fault," Brittany's father said. "When I was here none of this went on. She didn't ingest as many pills as they thought but still watching her get her stomach pumped was a warning. I need help."

"I remember the look on her face," Dawn said. "She was all red. She was crying, tears coming down her face. 'Why would you do this? Nothing in life is that bad.'"

Brittanee would be forced to see a counselor after the suicide attempt. Still, things seemed as if they were a mess on the home front. Her parents were separating and her mother was losing her home. But she would resume her studies at school and excel on the soccer field.

"She was fast," her father said. "Her coach would say he'd never seen a girl that fast."

By the time Spring Break rolled around in, she was ready to go on an adventure with some of the older kids she knew. It was a long-standing tradition for Rochester students to go to Myrtle Beach for vacation. Britt wanted to enjoy the night life and lay out in the beach, so when one of her older friends asked if she wanted to come along she didn't hesitate.

She asked her mother first and the idea was immediately shot dawn. Dawn Drexel did not know any of the friends that would be taking Brittanee.

"She asked me and I said 'no'," Dawn recalled. "Then she went to talk to her father. She would play us both. She would say Mom said 'no' but Dad said 'yes.'"

Brittanee was determined to go. She pleaded with her mother once again and was turned down. Angry, the two got into a fight and Britt would call her boyfriend to come pick her up.

Brittanee decided to fool her mother. She told her mother that she wanted to stay at a friend's house nearby for a couple of days. Dawn reluctantly agreed but Brittanee headed off to South Carolina instead.

Dawn believed that someone had offered her something, like a "modeling job or some other kind of ruse" to get her to go down there. She had aspirations of being a model as well as getting into cosmetology. With her striking good looks, she would be a shoo-in for success in the modeling profession.

"Her biological father was Turkish," Dawn said. "She had a very European look."

Defying her mother, Brittanee would visit her boyfriend at his workplace and tried to entice him to come along. The young man declined, stating that he had to work.

Brittanee then left with her older friends Jennifer Oberer, Phillip Oberer and Allana Lippa to Myrtle Beach. Jennifer was twenty-one years old. Her brother Phillip would be charged with rape in an unrelated case (charges would be dropped) in 2010. It is believed that these were considered the 'cool kids' and that Britt wanted to hang out and be liked by them.

Britt texted her boyfriend numerous times throughout the trip, telling him about the ambience. She expressed her love for the hot weather, palm trees and the happy vibe of young people finally away from parental supervision. But according to friends and family, Brittanee didn't know the older kids that well.

She also called her mother and lied, telling her that she waswatching movies at a friend's house.

CHANGE OF HEART

Britt hit the clubs with her friends and her mood quickly changed. Her friends began using a lot of drugs and she didn't want any part of that scene. She went off by herself, checking out the local shops and walking down the beach.

She then met up with a friend from Rochester, a man named Peter Brozowitz. He was also in town and staying at the Blue Water Resort with his own group of friends; Matthew Abrams, Philip Watson, Keith Cummings, and Anthony Schimizzi. The 20-year old Brozowitz was a "club promoter" who got Brittanee into Club Kryptonite. The next morning, she would meet Peter again at the beach.

The next day, Brittanee called her younger sister and told her that she's at the beach. Her sister believed she's at the local beach which is only twenty-minutes away. Britt then has a friend to impersonate the parent of the friend get on the phone to talk to her mother. The friend assured Dawn that everything was okay.

Britt then got back on the phone with her mother.

"I'll see you tomorrow," Britt said. "I love you and I'll see you tomorrow."

It would be the last time Dawn would ever speak to her daughter.

THE MYSTERY OF WHAT HAPPENED THAT NIGHT

Brittanee decided she would meet up with her friend Peter that night. She borrowed a pair of shorts from a friend and headed out. She texted her boyfriend John, telling him that she's having a miserable time and that she doesn't like the people she went down with. Apparently, they were 'mean-girling' her after she didn't do drugs with them.

She then received a text from her friend who stated that she wants her shorts back. Irritated, Brittanee walked back to the hotel to return the item.

At least that is what her friends say happened as Britt would disappear into the night.

John then became worried when Britt did not text him back. He texted her a few more times, waited, received no answer then he threatened to tell her mother that she's in South Carolina if she doesn't respond back.

Convinced that something is wrong, John calls Dawn at home. He explained that Brittanee is in Myrtle Beach.

Dawn went livid but her anger soon turned to concern when Britt didn't respond to her own texts or calls.

Everyone in Brittanee's family was notified. Something was wrong. Terribly wrong.

The next morning Dawn, her parents and John all made the trek to Myrtle Beach to try and look for Brittanee.

THE SEARCH BEGINS

Police in Myrtle Beach were notified and questioned the friends that Britt had been staying with. Their answers were all the same, they had not seen Brittanee since last night. Police also turned to Dawn, questioning her about Brittanee's state of mind.

Would she run away? Had she done this before?

There was no indication that Brittanee had motivation to do such a thing. Nor did they have any reason to believe she was doing a lot of drinking or drugs.

With no other leads, detectives turned their eyes on the last person to have seen Brittanee, Peter Brozovitz.

Peter would make an appearance on the Dr.Phil show and proclaim his innocence. He stated that they were in his hotel room watching the Yankees-Red Sox game when Brittanee was engaged in a texting argument with Jen Oberer who wanted her shorts back.

He said she didn't have a problem with walking a mile back to her own hotel.

Brittanee's parents were on the show and berated Peter for not "being a gentleman" and driving her back to the hotel. They also found it suspicious that Peter and the rest of Brittanee's friends did not do more after she was missing.

"I had spoken with Peter that morning," Dawn said. "He was giving me three different scenarios...It's fishy."

Peter responded angrily, stating that he was 'being thrown under the bus.' The innuendos were clear, that even if he had nothing to do with Brittanee's disappearance, she went missing because he didn't look out for her.

What is suspicious is that Peter had abruptly left Myrtle Beach with his friends around 2 a.m, five hours after Brittanee had vanished. They left clothing behind in their hotel room and looked to have been in a rush.

Upon his return to Rochester, Peter hired a defense attorney.

Peter had told investigators that she left his room shortly upon arrival to return the pair of shorts to her friend. The detectives got a hold of the surveillance camera from the hotel and verified Peter's story. At precisely 8:48 that evening she was seen leaving Peter's hotel to return back to her own hotel. She should have shown up on a traffic camera about fifteen minutes away but she never made it that far. She was abducted somewhere along that street.

Police continued to question Peter. The young man stated that one of his friends was told by his mother to return home immediately. This story was corroborated and law enforcement did not pursue the matter any further.

Instead, they now focused on Britt's cell phone.

Britt's last text message to her boyfriend was around 8:58. Ten minutes after she had left the hotel she texted "I'm packing and going to sleep probably."

This would be the last outbound message she sent as then John began texting her repeatedly with no answer back.

But the calls she received from John and her friends were pinged by her cell phone. Every time a friend called, her cell phone communicated with the nearest tower.

In looking at her cell phone records, she was moving southbound. The last ping was received at the Poleyard boat landing.

Fifty miles away from Myrtle Beach and two counties over.

Whoever abducted Brittanee knew exactly where they were going. The place was isolated, a rural country islet that only fishermen or locals would know about.

This was not the kind of place a seventeen-year-old girl would go to on Spring Break.

The investigators launched their search in the area that was about four miles in radius. Unfortunately, the terrain was treacherous. Alligators, wild hogs, snakes and biting insects the size of golf balls populated the area looking for their next meal.

Four-wheelers were brought in to keep the alligators away from the sniffing cadaver dogs. Investigators came to the site armed to shoot any wild hogs that came near.

"If her body is here," one investigator told Dawn in an ominous tone. "She would be eaten within six hours."

The search was frantic in the beginning but investigators seemed to lose hope after a few days passed. Britt's family returned home to Rochester with sunken hearts.

Brittanee's little brother chastized her friend upon their returning, stating "I thought you were bringing Brittanee back!"

Eight months later, police still had no promising leads. They would get an anonymous tip to check out an area a few miles north of the original search area near the Scantee River.

Once again, they came up with nothing. But a couple out fishing found a pair of sunglasses that looked as if they would belong to a teenage girl.

Neither her parents nor her boyfriend recognized the sunglasses as belonging to Brittanee. A DNA test was performed on the glasses and nothing was found.

Her mother continued to believe that she's alive.

"I think she was taken and held against her well," Dawn said. "I think she has become the victim of human trafficking."

Investigators and reporters shot down the notion, however. Typically, human trafficking occurs where the victim has a language barrier and Myrtle Beach was not exactly a hot bed for that type of crime. The police did not rule it out but it is low on their list of possibilities.

From 1997 to 2010, South Carolina has reported 12 cases of documented sex tracking. All were women, according to Doors to Freedom, an organization that helps victims of sex trafficking.

A few months later, police would receive some cell phone footage of Brittanee shot by a young man she had met. There were a group of teens antagonizing her and she wanted the young man's help to hang out with her so they would stop. He shot some footage of her sitting by herself, texting her boyfriend. He has since been cleared of any suspicion as he did have an alibi.

Pressed for suspects, law enforcement looked at every possible lead.

Three years later, authorities identified fifty-one year old Raymond Moody as a person of interest. They obtained a search warrant for a Georgetown motel room where Moody rented out at the time of

Brittanee's disappearance. They noted that Moody had received a traffic ticket in Surfside beach just one day after Brittanee went missing.

Moody was a a registered sex offender, having raped a nine-year old girl in 1983. He was released in June of 2004. But Moody did not cooperate with investigators and remained tight-lipped under interrogation.

He is also a suspect in the case of Crystal Soles who disappeared in January of 2005.

"We've heard his name before," Dawn Drexel said. "It's a possibility the cases are connected. We don't know what happened to Crystal or Brittanee."

Moody lived in an area where Brittanee's cell phone last pinged. He was referred to as "Mr.Clean" because of his resemblance to the bald character in the Mr. Clean commercials. He has not been mentioned in any police reports since 2012, however.

The FBI would get involved and offer their belief that Brittanee was abducted and taken to a "stash house" where she was raped and then murdered. Her body was then wrapped in plastic and she was thrown into an alligator pit where her body would presumably be eaten.

This narrative was offered by FBI Agent Gerrick Munoz who obtained the informaton from an inmate named Taquan Brown. Brown is serving a 25-year sentence for a different case but stated he was present during Britt's last moments.

He said he had seen Britt when he visited a "stash house" which was a moniker used by drug dealers to describe a place where they stashed weapons, money or drugs.

Brown stated that Taylor picked Britt up in Myrtle Beach and took her to McClellanville. Once there he "showed her off, introduced her to some other friend that were there...they ended up tricking her out with some of their friends, offering her to them and getting a human trafficking situation."

The stash house was in the McClellanville area, the last location where Britt's cell phone was pinged.

Brown told the officials that he saw Da'Shaun Taylor, who was 16 years old at the time, and several other men "sexually abusing Brittanee Drexel."

Brown then claimed he went to the backyard to give Da'Shaun's father money.

During this time, Britt tried to escape. She was caught by one of the men who "pistol whipped" her across the head. She was then taken back inside the house.

Brown stated that he heard two gunshots and then saw the woman being wrapped up and removed from the home.

The FBI agent revealed that "several witnesses" have told him that she was dumped in a pond that was filled with alligators.

Taylor has since been convicted of robbery in 2011 and could face a life sentence. He stated that he knows nothing of Britt's case and with the lack of evidence he has not faced any charges in her disappearance.

Chad Drexel, however, thinks Taylor may have been involved.

He recalled a time when he was out handing out Brittanee's missing person fliers and handed it to Taylor who was in his car.

"I gave him the flier," Chad said. "He had a car full of brothers, friends. He handed the flier to one guy in the back seat. They all laughed and then drove away and threw the flier out the window."

"I got mad. I said 'There's something about this guy...'"

After the information was released to the public, Taylor's mother, Reverend Joanne Taylor, immediately defended her son.

She stated that he had already served his time for the robbery (a McDonald's restaurant) and that he was a "great kid" that was only 16 years old at the time of Brittanee's disappearance. During her son's hearing, Taylor's mother took the stand and said the following:

"And I want to say that at the time of this alleged abduction, he was 16 years old. I was never a mother thatwould let my kids run loosely, and definitely not with the father, you know, out to do things. I kept great hold on him. I am a pastor of a church. They were in church, they had a strict bedtime, I knew every place that they went. MyrtleBeach would not be a place that he would go at the age of 16. So I just, you know, I ask for your fairness, I ask for, you know, the correct justice in this case. And know that he is not a flight risk. I mean, I teached them good values, I instill in them what few things that have happened, they have exemplified overall what I've taught them. He is not, you know, a flight risk or anything.

Chad Drexel read the testimony and immediately took to his own Facebook page.

I would like to set the record STRAIGHT with a STRONG REPLY to Joan Taylor's comments to the Post Courier in South Carolina this past Friday.

Based on evidence the FBI and the Myrtle Beach Police department has gathered, along with FACTS and SPECIFIC INFORMATION gathered from a team of Private Investigators that I HIRED to work with local law enforcement actively during the case (which will SOON COME TO LIGHT) – we have no doubt Timothy Da'Shaun Taylor played a significant role in the abduction and murder of my daughter.

Of course the mother of Timothy Da'Shaun Taylor is going to defend her son – as a father I can understand a need to defend your children. What I DON'T understand is defending your children when you must KNOW the truth. Her assumptions and words stated have been verified INCORRECT and couldn't be farther from the TRUTH. We know Timothy Da'Shaun Taylor was witnessed by others (Witnesses NOT IN JAIL) with my daughter – we are just praying that they do the RIGHT thing and stop forward with what they know. Additionally he has been seen and followed to the EXACT area where my daughter's DNA was found. Joan Taylor claimed that the FBI and government are falsely accusing her son because of witnesses IN JAIL?! Well, we have other specific evidence, that I can NOT disclose at this time for the safety of my daughters case, which corroborates these testimonies!! Timothy Da'Shaun Taylor is KNOWN to be involved in dog fighting, bringing drugs to parties, and raping women (mostly Caucasian young women) he either picks up UNWILLINGLY or friends of friends that end up being drugged and taken there. This IS ONLY THE BEGINNING!! There is a TON more "EVIDENCE and HORRIBLE INFO" we would like the PUBLIC in that area be aware of for their safety, but we are unable to disclose at this time.

WITHOUT A DOUBT ....Timothy Da'Shaun Taylor is a suspect in my daughter's Disappearance and Murder! My family and I will be following the FBI's requests to keep specific details in our daughter's case under wrap until THIS HORRIBLE PIECE OF TRASH goes to Prison for Life. After the guilty verdict, we will be happy to dispel these fairy tales that are being spun by Timothy's family. It is disgraceful the way this FAMILY and their FRIENDS are supporting and claiming innocence of a "PROVEN" FELON without even looking at the evidence presented and the FACTS surrounding the case.

Also adding this PIECE OF TRASH photo so everyone can see WHO HE IS!

On March 25th, 2017, FBI agents called Dawn Drexel to inform her they may have located Brittanee's remains. They are now searching an area 45 miles north of their previous search spot.

After two days, however, they gave up the search.

The case is ongoing.

THE STRANGE DISAPPEARANCE OF PATRICIA MEEHAN

NATHAN NIXON

Patricia Meehan Disappearance

The story of Patricia Meehan is a very strange and puzzling one. She seemingly disappeared into the night with little reason. The case has remained unsolved since 1989. With few witnesses, the full events are sketchy at best. What is well known about this case is that our culture has seemingly thought of every possible scenario to explain what happened to her. To understand and possibly solve the case, understanding the person that Patricia Meehan was is of paramount importance.

Patricia Meehan was never afraid of change. Her path of life took her all over the United States and to nearly every type of region. She was born on November 1, 1951 in Pittsburgh, Pennsylvania. She lived a typical life. She was said to have been "the perfect child" by her loving parents and by all who knew her. She had great ambition to see the world and to attack life with a smile. Socially she was on the same level as her peers. When she decided to attend college in Oklahoma City, Oklahoma, no one was really surprised. That was who Patricia was. That is exactly what she did.

She studied early childhood development and earned her degree in four years of college study. Again, she was living the American dream and successfully setting up a future to thrive. She made many friends in Oklahoma, even though it was a foreign place to a young woman from Pittsburgh. She took up a career in early childhood caregiving in Oklahoma and thrived in the profession for nearly 10 years. She was unhappy, or perhaps, unfulfilled in her work. She sporadically spoke with her family and a few friends from back home in Pennsylvania at the time. People knew Patricia to take risks. She was never afraid to change her outlook if it meant a new adventure or perhaps a new challenge lay ahead. In 1985, she made a major life change that would, effectively, lead to her ultimate disappearance.

She had informed her parents in the years prior that she wanted to become involved in animal care. She made this a reality when she moved to Bozeman, Montana in 1985. She moved alone. Patricia was not married and had left her simple, safe life behind in Oklahoma to pursue a career as a ranch hand. While this major career shift was motivated to start a happier life, it ultimately didn't always pay the bills. She worked numerous odd-jobs in the industry and could successfully make ends meet on her own. She continued this new lifestyle for four years in Bozeman, Montana.

The last person that can be fully confirmed to have seen Patricia Meehan alive was her landlord. Meehan's landlord reported to police investigators later that she seemed much more hyper than normal. This struck the landlord as extremely odd for the normally mellow, collected Patricia. Nonetheless, there were absolutely no problems between the two in any way. Patricia always paid her rent and was an "overall great tenant" to have.

The evening of April 20, 1989 is one of great speculation as to what really happened. The testimony of Peggy Bueller has always been a key component to the theories of Patricia's disappearance.

At approximately 8:05 P.M. Peggy Bueller and her father were traveling west bound on Montana State Highway 200. They were passing through the tiny town of Circle, Montana. To their surprise, they could see a set of vehicle headlights heading straight at them up ahead. A vehicle heading east was driving on the wrong side of the road. Peggy managed to swerve onto the shoulder and avoid a head-on collision with the opposing driver. The car that had been following behind Peggy was driven by an off-duty police dispatcher named Carol Heitz. Unfortunately for Carol, she was not able to swerve and avoid a collision.

Peggy Bueller had pulled over and gazed in her rear-view mirror in time to see the collision with the car driven by Carol Heitz. Thankfully, no injuries occurred in the accident. The story is very odd and somewhat eerie from this point. Just after impact, Carol Heitz emerged from her vehicle unharmed. She was shook up, but suffered no major injury. Being a police dispatcher, her first concern was for the other driver. The car that was traveling east bound was driven by Patricia Meehan. Patricia was next to emerge from her car after the impact. She stood in the middle of the road, and proceeded to slowly approach the car of Carol Heitz. According to Heitz, Patricia Meehan did not utter a single word. "She approached me calmly and silently," Heitz reported. "She seemingly stared directly through me from the moment she began to approach me."

Peggy Bueller remained in her vehicle and observed what was taking place. What she observed was "one of the strangest acts" she had ever seen. Peggy and Heitz agree that Patricia climbed over a fence just off of the road after she passed by Carol. She took only a step after getting over the fence and turned back around to stare upon the accident. She made no noise or any sort of expression. She stood there for at least two minutes. Heitz described Meehan as someone who seemed to be observing the accident scene rather than someone who had been involved in the accident. After a few short minutes, Meehan turned around and walked into a secluded Montana field into the pitch dark night. This was the last confirmed sighting of Patricia Meehan. By the time police arrived to sort out the accident, the whereabouts of Patricia were unknown. Peggy and Carol gave the exact same story in separate interviews with investigators. As eerie as the accident had unfolded, it had ended quietly and abruptly. Patricia Meehan was officially gone.

Peggy Bueller quickly drove into town when Patricia disappeared into the night. Her father stayed with Carol Heitz at the scene of the accident. Peggy reached a phone within ten minutes and alerted the authorities. When police arrived, an extensive search of the field where Patricia was seen walking away to turned up nothing. It only took police 15 minutes to identify the then mystery woman as Patricia Meehan after they ran the license plate of the vehicle. She was a registered member of the Bozeman, Montana community and had no criminal record. This was shocking to police who had assumed the woman left due to the fact that police would be arriving to the scene to investigate the accident. This posed the burning question that is still unanswered of why this woman would leave the scene of the accident if she had no criminal record.

Police made efforts to investigate the field immediately following the accident. Police discovered a tennis shoe about a mile into the field that had been accompanying a trail of footprints. The shoe matched what would have been the approximate size of the foot of Patricia Meehan. Oddly enough, the tracks seemingly disappear. Due to darkness, the investigation was suspended until the following morning of April 21. When police arrived to further check for a trail, the footprints led to nothing. The terrain had an influence in this as well as the fact that the actual shoe prints were gone, likely due to Patricia going barefoot at this point in her walk. Police had no leads.

There were two major theories that investigators had arrived at to this point. The first was the most likely. They believed that Patricia had hitchhiked from a small rural road in the area with a trucker. This could obviously not be confirmed, however the lack of a body, further clothes or footprints, as well as a lack of any whereabouts in surrounding cities points to this to be the likely case. The second theory they had suggest that she stowed away in a hay truck in the area and accomplished the same thing. This proved later to be unlikely as no hay trucks were confirmed to be in the field or in the immediate area.

The Meehan family arrived to Montana from Pittsburgh in the day following the accident. They distributed over 2,000 missing person flyers in the surrounding Montana towns and provided police with valuable information. The flyers turned up numerous calls, however none of these would lead to finding Patricia. Over 500 local volunteers searched the mountainous terrain around the accident site in an effort to possibly locate Patricia. For days, people walked the area. Some even brought dogs to perhaps catch a scent trail. These searches turned up absolutely nothing. There was no evidence of human activity in the mountains, and there were no evidence of a body or struggle in the surrounding area. Patricia had seemingly disappeared without a trace after taking a path into a secluded field. Perhaps the events in the days and weeks prior could shed some light into who Patricia was and things she had been recently going through.

The Meehan family revealed to police that Patricia had been going through some dark times in the past couple of months. Patricia was somewhat at a dead end and was feeling lost. She had asked her parents if she could return home in an effort to get back on track. Her parent's agreed, but only if she see a psychologist leading to coming home. Patricia agreed. She was diagnosed as suffering from depression. Ironically, she had an appointment with her psychologist the morning after the accident on April 21. She obviously never made this appointment.

Police also were suspicious as to why Patricia was even in this part of the state anyway. She had an appointment in Bozeman, Montana for the next morning. Bozeman was where she was living. The direction of travel she was taking at the time of the accident was in the opposite direction of Bozeman. Investigators asked the Meehan family if they had any idea where she may be going or what she was doing in this remote part of Montana. They had absolutely no idea. It was evident to police that she had no intention of returning to Bozeman to make her appointment the next morning. But could there be more to this part of the story?

The Meehan family had a roll of film developed that had been found in Patricia's car the night of the accident. The film was fully used. There were numerous pictures of nature. Beautiful countryside and the secluded area that Patricia loved. There were also numerous pictures of animals, specifically horses, that Patricia had devoted her life to in the recent years. Patricia's family stumbled across one picture that was quite alarming. A random picture that Patricia had taken in front of a mirror. She had a very confused look on her face and seemed lost. Investigation of the picture by mental professionals led some to believe she could have been suffering from amnesia. This could obviously not be proven, but would go further in explaining the odd behavior she displayed that night. Some of the investigators pointed to this as a possible reason that she was driving away from Bozeman and was 300 miles away from home. Could she simply have forgotten how to get home? Could her mental health had gotten that bad?

Patricia had been driving on the wrong side of the road and made no effort to swerve. Police drew two possible conclusions to this fact. The first was that she was so far lost in amnesia that she simply didn't think she was doing anything wrong or perhaps forgot the basic rules of driving. The second was that she was possibly trying to harm herself or had gotten so careless that the results were not clearly thought through. These are obviously speculation and will never be proven one way or the other. The mental health of Patricia was most assuredly in a low place.

The roll of film that was developed also proved something else to investigators and the Meehan family. Socially, she was in a dark place also. Out of every picture that had been developed, not one of them featured people that weren't named Patricia Meehan. This is clearly not the norm. Patricia had mentioned that she had had a few boyfriends since arriving in Montana, but nothing serious and committal. She had previously mentioned to her parents that she had become lonely and never really made any friends in her new home. This could help to explain the depression and possible mental health issues that she had developed.

Over the last 25 years, there have been over 5,000 reported sightings of Patricia Meehan. Through all of this, only 3 of those do police feel could be Patricia or are even likely to be her. In the days following her disappearance, there were some interesting leads that were generated by the public calls on the missing person flyers.

On May 4, 1989 just two weeks after the accident, a strong lead was generated out of Luverne, Minnesota. Out of all of the possible sightings, this is considered by police and those surrounding the case to be the most likely sighting of Patricia. A police officer in Luverne claimed to have seen Patricia sitting in a Hardee's restaurant by herself. For over five hours, she was sitting in corner booth drinking water. She remained until closing time, and then proceeded to walk to a nearby 24 hour diner. Here, the officer questioned her. The woman refused adamantly to give her name. She first said that she was from Colorado, and later said she was from Israel. The major problem with all of this is that the officer could not detain her. She had done nothing wrong. However, he left without further checking to identify her. This was perhaps the best chance to obtain Patricia if this indeed was her. The officer left and where this mystery woman went next is unknown.

Another interesting sighting occurred on May 19, 1989. This is nearly one full month after the accident. A waitress at a local restaurant in Bozeman, Montana reported seeing Patricia eating there. She informed police that Patricia at in a hurry and said she had to go shopping at 9 A.M. She said she was polite, but did seem to be displaying odd behavior. Another waitress on the same shift also reported seeing her. This waitress said she was talking to herself and seemed disoriented. Patricia left the restaurant and again, no attempts were really made to investigate who she really was.

The theories that surround this case are perhaps the most interesting in the current media. If Patricia was alive today, she would be in her late 60's. This would obviously make her hard to identify in the general public. This leads to the first theory.

The first, and generally most believed theory, is that Patricia simply wanted another fresh start. She had done this in the past, albeit in a much less drastic way. She wanted a fresh start after high school, so she attended college in Oklahoma City, Oklahoma. She wanted a career change and a change of passion nearly 10 years after she started her career, so she moved to Bozeman, Montana and became a ranch hand. Many feel that she again wanted a career change and a life change at this point in her life. Turning to her parents, they gave her an ultimatum to see a psychologist before she came home. The theory suggest that she wasn't happy with her family about this. She obtained her fresh start by planning an event that would allow her to vanish into the unknown.

What better place to accomplish this than a secluded highway in rural Montana where she could simply walk away.

This theory goes on further to explain that she had walked across the field and met up with someone who would drive her away. This theory doesn't sound too crazy at this juncture. The who or why is unknown, but the basis of the theory is mostly sound. Where she would have started this new life is completely unknown. But for a person who was struggling socially, not completely happy, and perhaps not enjoying the rural life as much as she had anticipated, this theory makes some sense.

The second popular theory is the more logical, medically supported theory. The collision that Patricia Meehan had was significant. While there were no injuries on the exterior, a concussion is without a doubt a possibility of this type of vehicle accident. Some believe that it was not amnesia to blame, but a concussion that would cause her to act so disoriented after the accident. The theory suggest that she exited her vehicle with a head injury and collapsed in the field shortly after beginning her walk into the night.

Montana is home to vast amounts of wildlife and has a very abstract climate. The night time temperatures in April in Montana typically are going to approach freezing. Anything under 50 degrees at altitude is going to be a severe situation for a minimally clothed, small woman with a possible head injury. The theory suggest that she was unconscious overnight and perhaps was eaten by animals, which would explain the lack of a body or any other evidence to her disappearance. It is for this reason that the theory is typically not accepted. Even with this, there would have been signs of this happening by one of the numerous volunteers or investigators in the following days.

The disappearance of Patricia Meehan has garnered national attention for the past 25 years. On November 1, 1989 the case was featured on *Unsolved Mysteries*. This would have marked the 38th birthday for Patricia.

Sightings are still reported on Patricia and a host of other in the United States. With each passing year, it is all too assuring that this case will never be solved. The lack of information on the case is puzzling. Those who choose to research the case will find that there is little information beyond the night of the accident and some significant reported sightings. All of these factors have led to a disappearance that has stumped police since that fateful night.

Patricia Meehan was an ambitious woman. She took risk in efforts to accomplish her goals and to get the most out of life. Anyone who ever knew her would say that she was a wonderful person with a positive view of the world. She loved her family dearly, and she loved her life deeply. She confidently left home to discover new opportunities on multiple occasions. It seems that life perhaps got too much for her in Montana. Maybe she just wanted to come home. Whatever the case, Patricia Meehan disappeared in April 1989, and has yet to be found. This beautiful young woman hasn't officially turned up in over 25 years. This tragic case may never be closed. A sure fact of the case is that Patricia was a sweet woman who didn't get in this situation by means of risky behavior or negative interactions. Likely, her disappearance can be attributed to a social low spot where she needed help that she didn't go through with getting. Maybe one day the truth of where her walk ultimately led will come out.

FOR MORE TRUE CRIME CLICK HERE[1]

---

1. http://www.pochepictures.com/truecrime.html

bonus:

Arlis Kay Perry was a newly married nineteen-year-old when she entered Stanford Memorial Church at Stanford University in the late night hours of October 12th, 1974. She would be found the next morning, the victim of a brutal murder in what appeared to be a ritualistic killing.

Her case has remained unsolved for the past forty-two years. Various rumors and theories abound as to who her murderer was. There is conjecture that she was the victim of the Son of Sam, the Zodiac Killer, the Death Angels and the Process Church.

The police never obtained solid leads on her case and it remains as much a mystery today as it was over forty years ago.

Who killed Arlis Perry?

EARLY LIFE

Arlis was born on February 22nd, 1955 in Linton, North Dakota to Marvin Dykema and Jean Van Beek. She usually wore glasses and had her hair straight. In the lone picture of her available online, her hair is wavy and she is not wearing glasses. This is an unfamiliar look for her and no one knows where or when the picture was taken. She was small, at 5'6" and weighing 110 lbs.

Arlis would graduate from Bismarck High School in 1973 where she was a cheerleader and a member of the Fellowship of Christian Athletes. She had a high school sweetheart, Bruce Perry, and they were both born again Christians. Bruce would be accepted into Stanford University upon graduation while Arlis would stay behind in Bismarck. She remained active in her church as a Sunday school teacher in the Bismarck reformed church.

Then she came into contact with people from the Process Church.

They were six young men that were renting a home across the street from her grandmother. Their names were Father Christian, Brother Thomas, Brother Joseph and three other men who were called "initiates."

The men tried to initiate Arlis into their religion but she soon became disenchanted with their belief system.

She realized that the were devil worshipers.

Arlis then made it a point to try and proselytize anyone who was involved in their church, leading them from Satanism into Christianity.

THE PROCESS CHURCH

The Process Cult became controversial in the early 1970s with its strong ties to the Manson family. Their belief system allowed them to worship both Christ and Satan. The church started in both Los Angeles and New York but branched out to North Dakota, as its leaders wanted the isolation of the hills and woods.

They would have meetings at the Hillside Cemetery in Bismarck and a wooded area behind Mary College. It was here that they would steal the dogs of people who lived in a nearby trailer park and sacrifice them in satanic rituals. People were complaining that they would find their dogs lying dead inside a "majick circle", their bodies badly mutilated.

MOVING TO CALIFORNIA

After graduation, Arlis would continue to participate in the Fellowship of Christian Athletes as a "huddle leader" as well as taking a job as a receptionist in a dental office. She would attend the local junior college for a year as she corresponded with Bruce Perry who was in his first year of studies at Stanford.

Bruce would return home and ask for Arlis' hand in marriage. She would accept and join him as he returned for his second year in Stanford's pre-med program.

Bruce's studies did not leave a lot of time for Arlis and she became a bit restless. She would take a job as a receptionist at a law firm to occupy her time during the day when Bruce would be away, finding work at the law firm Spaeth, Blase, Valentine, and Klein in Palo Alto.

The couple lived at the Quillen House in Escondido Village which was a campus housing unit for married couples.

Arlis got into the habit of taking nightly walks around the campus. Bruce worried for her safety and advised her not to. She stopped the practice until one night she wanted to get out of the home and mail off some letters.

DEADLY CHURCH VISIT

On October 12th, 1974 at around 11: 30 pm, Bruce and Arlis were walking on the Stanford campus. They would discover that the tire on Arlis' car had gone flat. They would have a minor argument as to who was going to take care of it. Bruce went back to the dorm and Arlis would go to the Memorial Church, telling Bruce that she wanted to pray alone.

Arlis entered and several people remembered seeing her. A security guard told her that it was almost midnight and the church was about the close up. She remained inside, however, and witnesses remembered seeing a "sandy-haired man" walk inside.

Arlis didn't return home after several hours and Bruce went out to look for her.

When he didn't find her, he called the police.

The next morning at around 05:45 am, security guard Steve Crawford would discover her body inside the church.

In Maury Terry's book, "Ultimate Evil", he described Perry's murder scene as follows:

"She was found lying on her back, with her body partially under the first pew on the left side of the alcove, a short distance from where she had been seen praying. Above her was a large carving which had been sculptured into the church wall years before. It was an engraving of the cross. The symbolism was explicit.

Arlis's head was facing forward, toward the main altar. Her legs were spread wide apart, and she was nude from the waist down. The legs of her blue jeans were placed upside down across her calves, purposely arranged in that manner. Viewed from above, the resulting pattern of Arlis's legs and the inverted blue jeans took on a diamond-like shape.

Arlis's blouse was torn open, and her arms were folded across her chest. Placed neatly between her breasts was an altar candle. Completing the desecration, another candle, thirty inches long, was jammed into her vagina. She had been beaten and choked. Death was due to her an ice pick being rammed into her skull behind her left ear, the handle protruding grotesquely from her head."

THE AFTERMATH

Security guard Crawford stated that he had locked up the church a little after midnight. He rechecked that the doors were still locked at around 02:00 a.m.

At 03:00 a.m. Perry had called the police and informed them that his wife was missing. The Santa Clara County Sheriff's went to the church and found all of the doors locked. Crawford would return to the church at 05:45 to unlock the doors and he found the west side door open.

The obvious suspect was Bruce Perry and police immediately went to brutally interrogate him.

"You knew your wife was having an affair so you killed her!"

Perry adamantly denied the questions. The police gave him a polygraph test which he passed.

Investigators would found two pieces of identifying evidence from the scene. They were able to collect a DNA sample which was found in semen near the body. The second was a bloody palm print found on one of the candles.

"It's a typical-if there is such a thing-sexual psychopathic slaying," Santa Clara County Undersheriff Tom Rosa said.

Rumors began to circulate around the campus. Some people were saying that Arlis was the victim of a satanist torture rite called the "Black Mass."

Rosa disputed the claim.

"It has no cult-like overtones," Rosa said. "It just happened to occur in a church."

There were no signs of a struggle. The detectives believed that Arlis was the victim of a "fast and sudden attack" as she entered the church around midnight.

Bruce would tell authorities that she often went there to pray when she was having problems.

SON OF SAM

Conspiracy theories would abound as the murder would go unsolved for many years. Some believe that Arlis was not murdered by a lone psychopath but by a satanic cult who stalked her from Bismarck, North Dakota.

Because of the way Arlis' body was positioned (legs spread with a candlestick in her breasts and vagina) people familiar with occult activity assumed that this was a ritualistic killing.

Fueling the speculation was some cryptic correspondence from David Berkowitz.

Berkowitz, the "Son of Sam" killer from New York City, had mentioned the Perry killing as he wrote authorities in North Dakota. He said that he had information on the killer, a man he referred to as "Manson II."

In 1979, five years after the murder, Berkowitz would send police authorities in North Dakota a book. In the margin, he had written: "Arlis Perry, hunted, stalked and slain, followed to California, Stanford Univ."

Berkowitz would claim that he was not the only person involved in the string of New York murders, hinting that he was part of a larger Satanic cult.

Detectives would later interview Berkowitz regarding Perry's murder but realized that he had "nothing of value to offer."

Those following the case, however, believe that Berkowitz should have been interrogated harder.

"Why would he make it up? He had no motive, no reason," crime writer Maury Terry asked. "He's confessed to three murders, he's not getting out."

The "Manson II" Berkowitz referred to was William Mentzer. Mentzer was suspected of being the head of the Son of Sam cult, had ties to the Manson family (although not to Charles Manson himself) and was suspected of being the Zodiac killer.

But was he responsible for killing Arlis Perry?

The answer may lie in the fact that at some point Mentzer was involved in a "hit squad" involving the Process Church. He allegedly performed assassin duties for the higher-ups who needed someone killed.

Interestingly, the serial murders of the Zodiac Killer stopped after Mentzer was in prison There were numerous parallels between the Zodiac Killer and Mentzer. Detectives believe that the Zodiac had military training. Mentzer had served in the Marines during Vietnam and killed ten people. Upon his return from the Vietnam War, the killings began in December of 1968.

The Zodiac would stab two of his victims with a bayonet style knife with rivets. Mentzer had a job where he was making rivets at a local aerospace company.

The Zodiac killer than began taunting the newspapers, sending them a diagram of a bomb while threatening to blow up a school bus. Mentzer later had a job driving a bus. He also had military training in demolition and plastic explosives. One of the survivors said that the killer spoke in a slow monotone with a drawl. Mentzer speaks the same way.

After a final letter to the press, the Zodiac mysteriously vanished in 1974.

Menzer would later be arrested for his role in the brutal murders of Roy Radin in 1983 and a prostitute/madam named June Mincher in 1984.

Radin had been shot more than twenty times in the head. Menzer would then put a stick of dynamite in Radin's mouth and blow off his face.

In the end, however, police didn't believe Menzer had probable cause to be the Zodiac killer and he would never be questioned for the death of Arlis Perry despite the rumors.

Crime writer Terry would investigate Perry's murder on his own and retrace her steps. He thinks that as many as four people were responsible for her death. He believes that the "sandy-haired" man who visited Perry at the law firm was a cult member from Bismarck, someone that she knew from the Process Church.

"She (Arlis) might have heard or seen something she shouldn't have," he said. "They may have feared she would expose them. Someone in Bismarck OK'd this, and someone had the hooks to get help on the West Coast," he said. "This was a pretty sophisticated operation."

BRUCE PERRY

Bruce Perry would complete go on to become a researcher in children's mental health and the neurosciences, becoming an internationally recognized authority in his field.

At Arlis's funeral, one of her law firm co-workers was confused when he saw Bruce. He thought her husband was a different man who had come into the workplace earlier. He witnessed her get into a "heated argument" with the man and assumed it was her husband. The co-worker described this man as "sandy-haired' which would fit the description of the man seen following Arlis into the church the night she was murdered.

Arlis would also note that there were two Bruce Perrys listed in the phone book. There is some speculation that Mentzer pretended to be Bruce Perry and had his name listed in the phone book. People from North Dakota would call and get him instead of Arlis' husband. He would then be able to finagle her whereabouts but subtly asking the family member the right questions.

This is one of the more far-fetched theories. It doesn't seem plausible that Menzer would go to the lengths of putting out a fake name and phone number just to coax Arlis' family and friends to call. Furthermore, he was a black-haired, mustachioed man who did not fit the "sandy-haired" man description.

But what is curious is that Perry's killing would be another instance of a series of unsolved murders that took place in and around the Stanford campus in the early 1970s.

A SERIAL KILLER AT WORK?

The murder of Arlis would be the fourth homicide on the Stanford campus in less than two years as well as the third incident in which the victim was a young woman out alone.

None of the murders were ever solved.

The killings started with Leslie Marie Perlov, a 21-year old Stanford history graduate who worked as a Palo Alto law librarian. She was found strangled to death on February 16th, 1973 in the foothills behind the campus. She had disappeared after leaving her workplace three days earlier.

Perlov's body would be found in a wooded gully where she had a scarf that was "wrapped tightly around her throat." There was no sign of a struggle where her body was found leading authorities to believe she walked there on her own volition.

She was not sexually assaulted but her skirt had been pulled up around her waist and her pantyhose had been stuffed into her mouth. While officers were searching for Perlov, they would find the body of Mark Rosvold, a twenty-five-year-old man out of Palo Alto. Rosvold was believed to have committed suicide the morning after Perlov was murdered. Perlov was last seen near the quarry gate of the Stanford campus, talking to a man with long blonde hair.

Seven months after the Perlov murder, physics student David S. Levine would be found stabbed to death on a walkway just east of the Meyer Undergraduate Library. The attack was estimated to have occurred between 1 and 3 a.m.

An early morning jogger would find the body of Levine. The young man had been stabbed fifteen times in the back and the side.

Like the rest of the murders, there had been no sign of struggle. The detectives believed that the young man was taken by surprise. Levine's empty wallet remained in his pants pocket and they ruled out robbery as a motive for the murder.

Levine was a straight-A student and called brilliant by his fellow students.

San Francisco Mayor Joseph Alioto believed that the murders were the work of a cult called the "Death Angels" who were suspects in the "Zebra" killings in San Francisco. Three months after the murder of Levine, a slaying took place on the UC Berkeley campus that was also rumored to be the work of the "Death Angels."

The Death Angels were a genocidal Black Muslim faction who mostly killed white people from October 1973 to April 1974. They were compromised of four black men: Manuel Moore, Larry Green, Jessie Lee Cooks, J.C.X Simon. The group committed at least 15 murders according to Wikipedia. Author Clark Howard estimates the group to be responsible for as many as two-hundred seventy deaths.

The Death Angeles would use .32 caliber pistols to shoot their victims point blank, however. They would take people by surprise but there were not any instances where they used strangulation or a knife for the initial attack as was the case for Perlov and Levin.

On March 24th, 1974, Janet Ann Taylor was strangled while hitchhiking to her La Honda home after visiting a friend on the Stanford campus. Her body was found early the next morning in a roadside ditch. Taylor was twenty-one years old and the daughter of former Stanford athletic director, Chuck Taylor.

Detectives would later concede that there were "similarities" between the Perlov and Taylor murders.

Both would be strangled although Taylor would be choked by hand instead of a scarf. Neither were sexually violated.

Both were barefoot when their bodies were found and wearing raincoats. Neither of the purses were on the person when their bodies were found.

"We really don't know who we're looking for," Sheriff's Inspector Rudy Siemssen said after the Taylor killing. "We have no motive. She apparently had no money in her purse, although you could speculate that robbery was a motive. It's a rough one."

WHO KILLED THEM?

None of the unsolved Stanford murders seem to be connected in terms of the method of killing. But, on the surface, they all were senseless and without motivation.

In the case of Arlis, there is mere speculation because of her conversations with the Bismarck Process Cult. The rumor is that someone from the cult, a leader or ordered assassin, came out to California because she tried to convert their members to Christ.

What is curious about the case is how the body was positioned. Arlis' pants were moved but placed on top of her body. The pants were positioned legs up, across her calves and her legs were spread apart. Her arms were in a crucifix position and the altar candle was shoved in her vagina.

Looking at her body from above, she was positioned in the Mason's symbol of Freemasonry. So this suggests that her murder was the work of someone involved in the Freemason cult or someone who was trying to make it look as if there was Freemason involvement.

It also appeared that Arlis may have known her killer. Her meeting with the "sandy-haired" man at work or the church may have been a scheduled meeting place. She was a devout Christian woman, used to doing the right thing, so it seems a bit odd that she wouldn't obey the security guard when he told her he was closing up the church.

The speculation is that she was meeting someone, probably the "sandy-haired" man. Who he was or how they came to meet is the question of the day. The problem is that the police failed to see the cult link in the killing, with some kind of warped religious undertones. How much of an evangelist was Arlis and who exactly did she speak with at the Process Cult in Bismarck?

The police were never interested in pursuing that line of thought.

There were rumors in Bismarck that well-known people were part of a satanic cult that performed all kinds of grisly rituals at Pioneer Park and the caves behind the University of Mary. One witness reported that they remembered seeing people come into town in priest's outfits. Only they weren't wearing white collars. They were wearing red collars and upside-down cross necklaces.

Jon Martinson, a former psychology professor at Bismarck State College, doesn't buy the theory that Arlis was stalked from Bismarck to California.

"I remember a lot of weird religious stories going on around here in that time," Martinson said. "Like covens dancing under the full moon and rituals taking place down by the river bottoms. But in her case, I think she was at the wrong place at the wrong time."

After Terry's book "The Ultimate Evil" came out, students around the Bismarck around began trolling around the University of Mary looking for any semblance of satanic cult activity. They found none but it became an urban legend around the town. The caves behind the University of Mary were eventually filled in.

Terry still firmly believes that Berkowitz knew something that the police didn't follow-up on. "It's very important to know that it was Berkowitz himself who raised the connection to (the University of) Mary, and he did it in late 1979 – nearly eight years before The Ultimate Evil was published," Terry said. "Nothing about the Mary (University of Mary) ties to Arlis' death was made public until the book came out. But Berkowitz knew about cult activities there all along. And I also confirmed that rituals had been occurring there in the 1970s."

Ken Kahn was one of the detectives who flew into Attica State Prison in New York to interview Berkowitz. The Son of Sam killer remained vague and didn't fess up to any details. This led Kahn to believe that Berkowitz was simply messing with the crime writer and knew nothing of the murder of Perry or anyone else at Stanford.

Martinson and Terry remain adamant that Berkowitz knows something as he was documented to have been in nearby Minot Air Force base before he committed his own murders. Martinson showed Berkowitz a series of photographs from people who Terry believed was involved with Perry's murder. Berkowitz identified one of the men in the photo as someone he had met during his satanic cult meetings in Minot.

FOREVER COLD

Detectives were hoping that with advanced DNA technology and handprint databases they would get a lead on the who left behind the semen and bloody handprint.

To date, there are still no leads.

Arlis' parents would stay in contact with the Santa Clara Sheriff's Department for more than thirty years.

Eventually, however, the sheriffs would stop returning their calls.

Arlis Perry's murder remains unsolved.